Study Testimonials

"I have known many of these Scriptures most of my life, and I didn't understand the level of love God placed within His Word to protect His daughters until I completed this study."

Deborah

"This study taught me that a woman's voice is powerful, and she can stand up, speak up, and show up for righteousness in God's Truth and HE will have her back!!"

Susan

"This transformative Bible study unpacks the lives of women and helped me understand the meaning behind God creating us and saying it was a good thing. It will open your eyes to see that God has given women purpose; He has given us a voice that matters and is most powerful when we use it; and that He has given us grace and mercy to stay in alignment and in unity with Him to experience blessings and favor."

Dr. Natalie Mayes Woods

"How good and amazing God is with us women. How good God has been with me."

Karen

"I matter as a woman. This study reminded me that I am valued, seen, and heard all the time by the Almighty."

Sabrina

"I learned through this study that God created my voice for me to use it to agree with His plans and purposes for my life."

Evelyn

Published by Market Refined Publishing,
An Imprint of Market Refined Media, LLC
193 Cleo Circle
Ringgold GA 30736
marketrefinedmedia.com

Bite-Size Bible Studies for Women.

All Scripture quotations, unless otherwise indicated, are taken from the King James Version (KJV). Scripture taken from the King James Version (KJV), is public domain.

Cover and Interior Design by Nelly Murariu at PixBeeDesigns.com
Manuscript Edits by Gleniece Lytle and Market Refined Media

Print ISBN: 979-8-9868023-3-6
Digital ISBN: 979-8-9868023-4-3
Library of Congress Control Number: 2022920863

First Edition: March 2023

Eve

The Importance of
a Woman and Her Voice

CATINA HARRIS

To my heavenly Father and
His darling Son, Jesus Christ,
my Savior and Redeemer—without
whom my life was withered, worn,
and weakened as a woman

Contents

Preface

I have been a Christian woman for many years, and I didn't fully understand God's love for His daughters until He revealed it to me. I have heard thousands of sermons, listened to hundreds of Bible studies, and attended many women's events, but I had never understood God's unique provision, calling, purpose, and freedom He designed for His women until I studied Eve and how she came to be.

As a wife and a mother, I experienced an emptiness and exhaustion that I didn't expect, and nothing in my faith arsenal prepared me for it. When I studied Eve's life, I learned that she also experienced an emptiness and exhaustion in both her marriage and motherhood. As I sought God and believed that He had more for my life, He led me to passages of Scripture about women, wives, mothers, and daughters who suffered, who endured trauma and abuse, and who triumphed regardless of what they had gone through.

I discovered that God's love is deeper, wider, and more unlimited than I thought it could be. He taught me that all women face certain inherent problems, and God has gone to great lengths to give women a foolproof strategy that brings deliverance, freedom, and promotes victory. This strategy consists of understanding the importance of a woman's worth, a woman's rest, and a woman's words.

God has done everything in His power to love, lift, lighten, and lavish His blessings onto His female creation. God has given women the power of rest, but women must take the responsibility to rest and receive all the benefits that come from this discipline to experience peace. God has also given women the power of worth and value, and it is inherent within womanhood. Women must place the same worth and value on themselves that God places on their lives. Lastly, God has given women His Word, and when we speak God's words and agree with Him, we are directed, protected, and live free.

As a woman, allow God to minister, heal, and bless you through this study.

Introduction

*E*ve: The Importance of a Woman and Her Voice* Bible study is a refreshing and affirming reminder to women of their importance to God, themselves, and others. It educates and enlightens women that their voices encompass what they speak, do, and believe. This study was designed to challenge women to use their God-given voice to speak up and create the good they want to see in the world.

This study engages women in a real and authentic way. It ministers to their core being and reveals truth about feminine strength that empowers and feminine struggles that have haunted women since the beginning of time. This study challenges and requires women to understand that, for them to be totally free, their voice is the key that God has given them to be used as a divine weapon that allows God's light and love to stand against the enemy.

The biggest battle any woman will ever face in life is the battle to rest in her God-given voice and authority, which is the authentic calling on her life. A woman's voice is more than what she says, it is also what she does and believes. A woman's voice is most powerful when what she says, what she believes, and what she does, agree. When a woman's words match her actions it fosters and births integrity. God desires every woman to use her voice to bring light, laughter, and liberty into her life.

Each Bible study session consists of a weekly thought that you can reflect on for the entire week. Daily reflections are also provided to help you retain the weekly thought by laying a deeper foundation of its present relevance and applicability. You will be challenged with summary questions that will help you reflect on and improve your life.

As you complete this study, you will have a better understanding of why God made woman, her divine purpose, and her worth in the earth. You will strengthen your brand, increase your stock, and experience a substantial rate of return on your life. The principles that await you as you delve deeper into the unsearchable riches of God's Word concerning woman in the study of Eve will reward you with priceless treasure that will continually bring you increase.

ENCOURAGEMENT TO ALL WOMEN

Every woman who completes this study will have inevitably made mistakes relating to her worth, value, rest, actions, deeds, and beliefs, just as Eve did. This study is written to encourage you that your mistakes are your markers in life to help re-route you in the direction God wants you to travel. Your mistakes don't disqualify you, limit you, or diminish you, but they make you stronger, wiser, and more sensitive to making right decisions.

When you read this study be encouraged, comforted, and hopeful that God gives women daily opportunities to make course corrections in life. If you have lived empty, fullness awaits you. If you have lived fearful, faith awaits you, and if you have lived insignificant, significance awaits you. All you must do is choose to use your voice to agree with God's purposes, plans, and promises for your life.

Be encouraged that God's grace and truth provide new opportunities each day to correct past wrongs. God has an abundance of love, forgiveness, and blessings for His daughters when we do the necessary work to atone. This study lays out foundational feminine truth that rest is a weapon that brings well-being to every woman. Goodness resides within every woman's heart, and a woman's voice is one of the most important powers on earth if she chooses to use it to align with the divine purposes that God has for her.

When you finish this study, you will have learned and understood the following:

- A woman was created by God's own hand, not a man's plan
- A woman deserves her husband's undivided loyalty; she must take priority
- A woman requires rest for complete and healthy growth
- A woman should never settle for less than a God-anointed and God-appointed man
- A woman's voice is most powerful when what she does, speaks, and believes agrees with God's Word.

WHAT MATERIALS DO I NEED?

 **Bible** Any translation of the Bible may be used with this study. It will help to provide context and greater clarity.

 **Notebook, Journal, Electronic Tablet** Having a paper or electronic journal will be helpful to record your answers to questions and to take extra notes that you may refer to later.

 **Pen or pencil** Thoughts are fleeting and having a pencil or pen available to capture insights and revelations will be extremely beneficial as you go through this study.

JOURNEY DEEPER INTO WOMANHOOD

How we see ourselves as women is very important, because how we see ourselves is how we will treat ourselves and how we will allow ourselves to be treated. The exercise below is a simple and quick way for you to get a clear picture of how you see yourself based on genuine facts and feelings you experience in life.

EXERCISE 1: Before you jump into week one, please take a moment to complete the simple exercise below. Review the chart and circle one word from each row that best describes how you see yourself today. Think about every area of your life and select the word that best describes you most of the time. Be honest, transparent, and authentic with each answer.

Example: Select **strong** if you feel strong in your family, career, and spiritual life. Select **weak** if you feel weak in your family, career, and spiritual life. You should select **strong** if you are balanced, respected, and honored in these areas, and you should select **weak** if you are anxious or stressed in these areas.

How do you currently think of yourself as a woman?

☐ Strong 🌿 ☐ Weak   ☐ Connected 🌿 ☐ Disconnected

☐ Independent 🌿 ☐ Dependent   ☐ Authentic 🌿 ☐ Conforming

☐ Kind 🌿 ☐ Unkind   ☐ Collaborative 🌿 ☐ Cautious

☐ Mature 🌿 ☐ Immature   ☐ Adventurous 🌿 ☐ Reserved

☐ Compassionate 🌿 ☐ Indifferent   ☐ Flexible 🌿 ☐ Rigid

☐ Content 🌿 ☐ Discontent   ☐ Restful 🌿 ☐ Worried

☐ Bold 🌿 ☐ Fearful   ☐ Respected 🌿 ☐ Disrespected

Isaiah 54:4-7

4 *Fear not; for thou shalt not be ashamed: neither be thou confounded; for thou shalt not be put to shame: for thou shalt forget the shame of thy youth, and shalt not remember the reproach of thy widowhood any more.*

5 *For thy Maker is thine husband; the Lord of hosts is his name; and thy Redeemer the Holy One of Israel; The God of the whole earth shall he be called.*

6 *For the Lord hath called thee as a woman forsaken and grieved in spirit, and a wife of youth, when thou wast refused, saith thy God.*

7 *For a small moment have I forsaken thee; but with great mercies will I gather thee.*

A Woman Was Created for Good, to Do Good, and to Be Good

Welcome to exploring the reasons why you were created as a woman and how God designed you to use your voice for His glory and tell His story of love in the earth. This Bible study takes you on a journey of the essential principles that every woman should understand about her existence so that she can thrive and live her best life.

All women need to understand that God loves them unconditionally, unequivocally, and irrevocably. He has provided blessings for their lives that are exceedingly, abundantly, above all that they could ask, think, or imagine according to God's power at work within them (Ephesians 3:20).

To understand your existence as a woman, you must first reflect on why God created the first woman and when, where, and how she came into existence. The answers to these questions are essential to finding truth and understanding God's purposes, plans, and promises for women today. Studying the geographical, cultural, and spiritual contexts of woman's creation will reveal insightful revelation about God's perfect will for women.

Many women believe lies about God and about life. They base their lives on lies that are prevalent in society. This study will introduce you to new truths about your role as a woman in the kingdom of God.

You will be joyfully surprised to learn that as a woman you are meant to be seen and heard. You are meant to use your voice to agree with God and courageously speak His truth over all lies that surface in your heart. Once you identify some common lies, you can embrace truth, admit truth, and live truth so you can have genuine authenticity in life.

The truth is, God made you equal to man in intelligence, in worth, and in value. Because woman was created from man, she is no less than man, and she is no more than man. She is equal to man and deserves to be treated with equity accordingly. God's Word clearly states that in Christ there is neither male nor female (Galatians 3:28), which really means in Christ God reconciles and unites all differences and uses them as strengths for the cause of advancing His kingdom. This study will help you lean into your womanhood and tap into God's goodness and glory for your life.

BACKGROUND AND BIBLICAL HISTORY OF THE FIRST WOMAN

And God saw the light, that it was good: and God divided the light from the darkness. . . . And God called the dry land Earth; and the gathering together of the waters called he Seas: and God saw that it was good. . . . And the earth brought forth grass, and herb yielding seed after his kind, and the tree yielding fruit, whose seed was in itself, after his kind: and God saw that it was good. . . . And God created great whales, and every living creature that moveth, which the waters brought forth abundantly, after their kind, and every winged fowl after his kind: and God saw that it was good. . . . And God saw everything that he had made, and, behold, it was very good (Genesis 1:4, 10, 12, 21, 31).

And the Lord God said, it is not good that the man should be alone; I will make him an help meet for him. . . . And the Lord God caused a deep sleep to fall upon Adam, and he slept: and he took one of his ribs, and closed up the flesh instead thereof; And the rib, which the Lord God had taken from man, made he a woman, and brought her unto the man. And Adam said, this is now bone of my bones, and flesh of my flesh: she shall be called Woman, because she was taken out of Man. Therefore shall a man leave his father and his mother, and shall cleave unto his wife: and they shall be one flesh. And they were both naked, the man and his wife, and were not ashamed (Genesis 2:18, 21–25).

A WOMAN WAS CREATED FOR GOOD, TO DO GOOD, AND TO BE GOOD

Genesis chapter 1 reveals how God looked at everything He created as very good. The light was good, the earth and the gathering of the seas were good, the earth bringing forth harvest was good, the dividing of day and night was good, and the living creatures were good. For the first time, we see something that wasn't good, and it was found in Genesis 2:18. God perceived it was not good that man should be alone. Interestingly, as soon as God determined and decided it was not good for man to be alone, He immediately focused on bringing a solution to fix the "not good" situation of man being alone.

What does this immediate response by God reveal about His character?

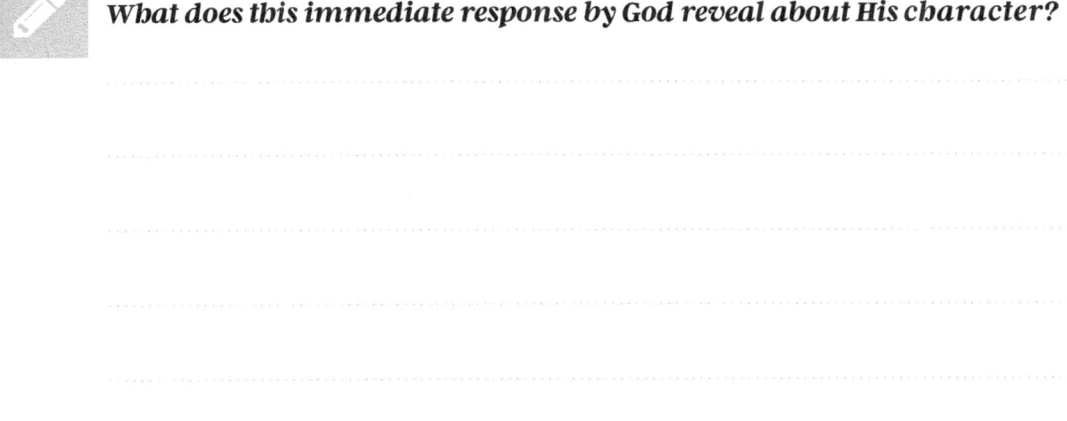

As we unpack the Scripture that states "it is not good that man should be alone," in Genesis 2:18, we can deduce that *woman was created for good, to do good, and to be good*, because it was not good for man on earth without her. Additionally, the Bible confirms this in Proverbs 18:22 where it tells us the man that finds a wife finds a good thing and obtains favor from the Lord. God created a good thing when He created woman. Now, it is important to note that a wife and a woman are not the same thing. However, the first woman, Eve, happened to be both a woman and a wife, and she was a good thing. All women are not wives, but all women are created for good regardless of whether they decide to be wives.

Genesis 2:18 gives us insight into why God created women—to bring good to the not good that exists in life.

How did God fix the (not good) situation of man being alone in the earth—what did He do?

WOMAN WAS GOD'S IDEA AND GOD'S DESIGN

The Bible spends a considerable amount of time on the first woman, Eve. I believe God wants people to understand the thought, the detail, and the planning He went through to design the first female. Additionally, I believe that God desires all to understand that creating a woman was God's idea, God's design, and God's plan. A woman wasn't man's idea, man's design, or man's plan.

God fashioned woman with His own hands. God made sure man was asleep when he created woman, so man wouldn't have any say in her appearance, her personality, her desires, and who she would be. Man was not allowed to comment on a woman's lips, hips, or fingertips, especially how big, how curvaceous, or how attractive each would be. Therefore, I believe God made sure man was asleep. (Your body was created for divine functionality, not human futility and folly.)

Why do you think God didn't allow Adam to have any opinions on what woman would look like or act like?

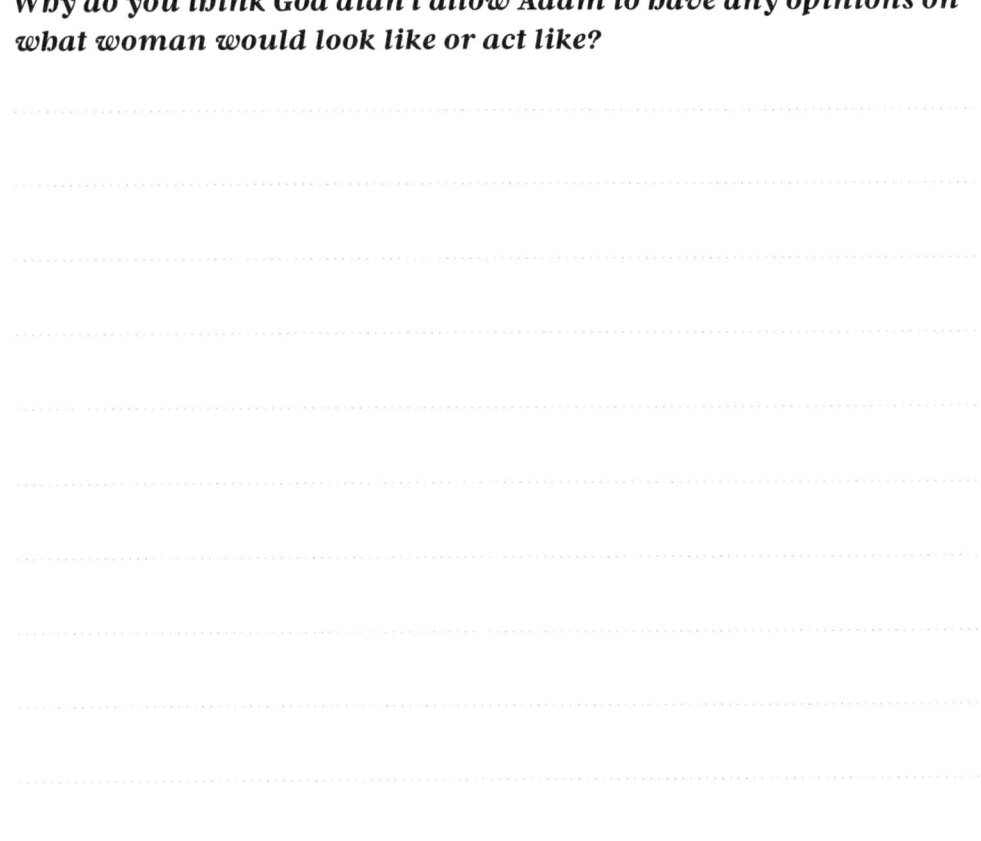

GOD ANOINTED AND GOD APPOINTED MEN

God didn't reach back into the ground when He created woman, but He reached into a God-anointed and God-appointed man to create woman. This particular detail gives critical insight into the importance of a woman having healthy male companionship and fulfillment in life. A woman walking in her anointed and appointed calling should be connected to men who are walking in theirs. It is imperative for women to unite, to connect, and to bond with these types of men, and the connection should be spiritual, not physical, to foster healthy growth. Remember, Adam was successfully functioning as a leader and a planner; he was a man who walked with God before woman ever came on the scene. Thus, the goal for a woman should not be to have *any* man, but to have a healthy relationship with a God-anointed and appointed man.

Why do you think God didn't create Eve like He created Adam, by reaching back into the ground?

GOOD OF WOMANHOOD

As we look back in history, we see the evidence of women who have brought good to life, by championing freedom for all, justice for all, and equality for all. For example, Fannie Lou Hamer, a civil rights activist, made the difference for God's people to get the right to vote in the deep south of Mississippi. Fannie brought good to the not good that existed in a racially unjust state like Mississippi. Fannie used her God-given voice, convictions, and beliefs to advance God's justice in the earth.

Similarly, Helen Keller made the difference for those who were born blind, deaf, and mute to have equal rights. Helen brought good in the form of education and awareness to the not good that existed for those who were marginalized and disadvantaged. She used her voice and her life to advance God's justice and to make a positive difference for those who had been left behind. Let there be no doubt that women were created to bring good to life. As a woman, you were created for good, to do good, and simply be good.

Week One

Thought of the Week

A woman was created for good, to do good, and be good,
because it was not good on earth without her

God created woman because it was not good for man to be alone without her. A woman brings good to situations that are not good in life when she is walking in her God-given purposes, plans, and promises.

DAILY REFLECTIONS

 Everything God made was very good until He realized it wasn't good that Adam was alone. This teaches that God reflected on His work and evaluated it, and His reflection allowed Him to observe opportunities for greater growth.

> *Two are better than one; because they have a good reward for their labour. —Ecclesiastes 4:9*

Daily Takeaway: Reflection is good

 God saw that it was not good that Adam was alone, and He quickly worked to solve it.

Daily Takeaway: Evaluation is necessary for growth

God looked to existing creation for a help meet, but He couldn't find anything suitable.

God looked within the Garden of Eden for a help meet before He looked inside Adam.

Daily Takeaway: Solutions to most problems are always closer than we think

 God custom designed woman to be a help meet to bring harmony to man on earth.

God used a rib to make woman and ribs protect, strengthen, and support the body.

Daily Takeaway: Woman was God's custom design to bring support, harmony, and strength to life.

 A woman exists by God's voice not by a man's choice, and a woman is a good thing.

Whoso findeth a wife findeth a good thing, and obtaineth favour of the Lord. — Proverbs 18:22

Daily Takeaway: A woman is good, and she's created to do good things

 God put Adam to sleep, so Adam didn't comment on woman's lips, hips, or fingertips.

Daily Takeaway: God designed woman completely

 God didn't reach back into the ground to create a woman. God reached into a God-anointed and a God-appointed man to create a woman.

Daily Takeaway: Women need God-anointed and God-appointed men to thrive

Week One

Summary and Reflection Questions

1. Do you believe that woman was created for good, to do good, and be good in the earth? Why or why not?

2. As a woman, what good are you bringing to life in your family and in your own personal life?

3. Can you think of biblical or historical women who have brought good to their lives? If so, list these women and their good deeds.

4. How did God react when he perceived it was not good that Adam was alone? How did God solve the problem?

....

....

....

5. Do you believe that God wants His people to react positively and immediately to things we perceive that are not good on earth?

....

....

....

6. Have you ever perceived that a situation or circumstance was not good, and immediately sought to bring good to the environment? If so, please describe the situation and how you brought good to it?

....

....

....

7. When you perceive something is not good, how do you generally react? Do you pray, act, or ignore?

....

....

....

....

8. Should we respond the way God did and focus on a solution to fix the not good in the earth, when we have the power to bring positive change?

9. If a woman was created from a God-anointed and God-appointed man, what does this indicate about the type of man women need in life?

10. What does it mean to you to be a custom design by God, to be fashioned and shaped for His plans?

11. Do you have any God-anointed and appointed male companionship in your life that's healthy and fulfilling? Why or why not?

12. How do you describe healthy male companionship that's God-anointed and appointed?

....

....

....

13. Are you intimidated or affirmed to know you were created for good, to do good, and to be good? Spend some time and reflect on your feelings.

....

....

....

14. Why do you think God used a rib to create a woman?

....

....

....

15. Before you studied this week's teaching, did you think of yourself as God's custom design? Why or why not?

....

....

....

JOURNEY DEEPER INTO WOMANHOOD

How we see other women is very important, because how we see other women is how we will treat other women. If we fail to see every woman's worth and value, we will fail to treat every woman with worth and value. The exercise below is a simple and quick way for you to get a clear picture of how you see other women based on genuine facts and feelings you experience in life.

EXERCISE 2: Before you jump into week two, please take a moment to complete the simple exercise below. Review the chart and circle one word from each row that best describes how you see other women. Think about the women in your life and select one word that best describes how you see the totality of women in society today. Be honest, transparent, and authentic with each answer.

Example: Select **strong** if you feel women are looked upon as strong in their families, careers, and spiritual lives. If you feel women are looked upon as **weak** in their families, careers, and spiritual lives, select weak.

How do you think of other women?

☐ Strong 🌿 ☐ Weak   ☐ Connected 🌿 ☐ Disconnected

☐ Independent 🌿 ☐ Dependent   ☐ Authentic 🌿 ☐ Conforming

☐ Kind 🌿 ☐ Unkind   ☐ Collaborative 🌿 ☐ Cautious

☐ Mature 🌿 ☐ Immature   ☐ Adventurous 🌿 ☐ Reserved

☐ Compassionate 🌿 ☐ Indifferent ☐ Flexible 🌿 ☐ Rigid

☐ Content 🌿 ☐ Discontent   ☐ Restful 🌿 ☐ Worried

☐ Bold 🌿 ☐ Fearful   ☐ Respected 🌿 ☐ Disrespected

Rest Is Essential to a Woman's Well-Being

And the Lord God caused a deep sleep to fall upon Adam, and he slept: and he took one of his ribs, and closed up the flesh instead thereof; And the rib, which the Lord God had taken from man, made he a woman, and brought her unto the man. Genesis 2:21–22

In Genesis 1, God brought order to chaos. He brought light to darkness, life to dust, and purpose to emptiness. Order was the key to establishing a healthy planet and humanity. God created Adam after He had brought order to the Garden of Eden.

God created woman in a place of rest and from a man at rest. Eve was birthed in an environment free from stress, anxiety, and strife. She was designed to thrive in this environment because it allowed her to rest in her true authenticity. A woman mentally thrives when her mind is at peace. Therefore, rest is essential to a woman's growth, development, and well-being.

Do you get the rest you need, spiritually, mentally, and physically?

Most women believe they are most powerful when they are working, but the truth is real power comes when a woman is resting in who she is. A woman should be resting in her working, resting in her parenting, resting in her waiting, etc. Resting is a spiritual discipline that provides power, and it should be entered into daily. Christ offers an invitation to us all to come and receive rest from Him, and His invitation should never be rejected (Matthew 11:28–30).

If rest is essential to a woman's well-being, then unrest will be the tool of the enemy to wreak havoc in a woman's life. The enemy will always send someone or something to disturb a woman's rest. The enemy desires for a woman's mind to be anxious. He desires for her personal life to be full of drama and chaos, and he desires for her to doubt herself constantly and consistently. But God's design of woman gives the greatest clue to help all women to live in a place of serenity—the Garden of Eden was filled with physical and spiritual peace. Therefore, you must cultivate relationships and environments that bring you rest and eliminate those that bring you stress.

Who and what do you have in your life right now that causes you unrest, anxiety, and steals your peace?

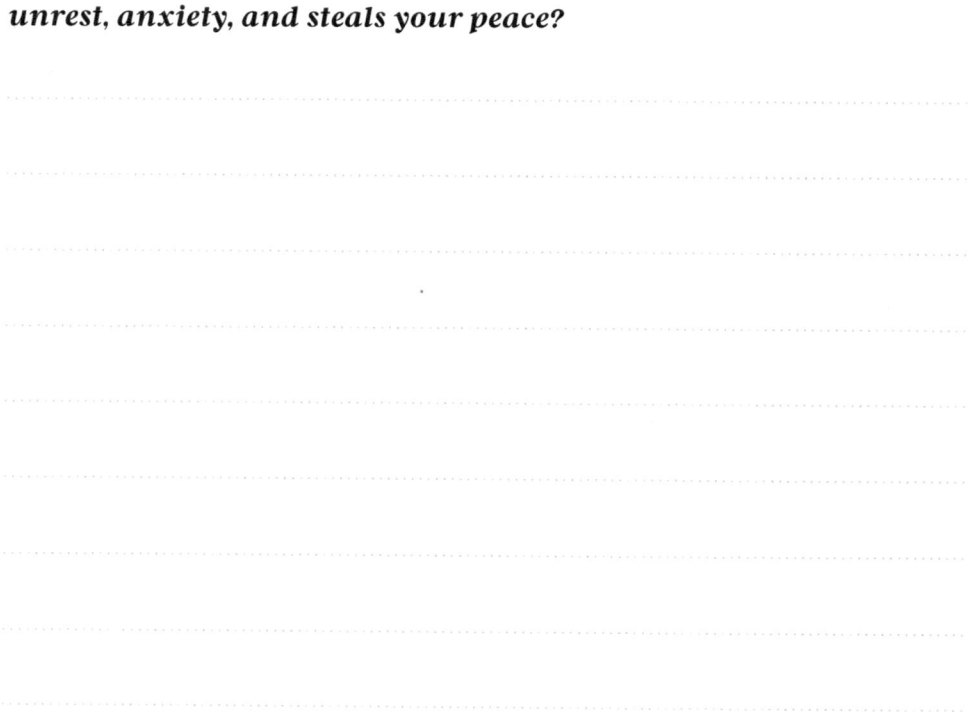

Eve was content, at rest, and at peace when she lived in the Garden of Eden with her hubby, until the enemy slithered in. I don't believe Eve understood the enemy came to steal her peace when he challenged her to eat from the Tree of Knowledge of Good and Evil. Additionally, I don't believe most women understand when the enemy is causing them to doubt their beliefs and doubt their abilities. Remember, God often uses people to speak blessings into our lives, and the enemy often uses people to speak curses into our lives. Just as God used Peter to speak truth and revelation that Jesus was the Christ, the enemy used Peter to rebuke Christ when He foretold of His death by way of the cross (Matthew 16:16–23). We have to be alert and attentive to the people we allow to speak into our lives so we are able to discern words that are life and words that are death.

Who and what do you have in your life that causes you rest, blessing, joy, and peace?

A WOMAN WAS CREATED TO SOLVE THE PROBLEM OF MAN BEING ALONE

Another interesting fact about God's creation of woman is that she was created as a solution to a problem. Adam never requested a companion, but God knew that without woman on earth it was not good for man. In other words, woman was the solution to God's search for a suitable help meet for Adam. *A woman was God's choice; she didn't occur because of a man's voice.* It is important to note that being alone is not a bad thing but being isolated is. If Adam had remained isolated in Eden, he wouldn't have been able to fulfill the commandment God gave him to be fruitful, multiply, replenish, subdue, and have dominion. Thus, God created purpose in companionship. Healthy companionship brings comfort, clarity, and connection.

The Bible specifically states that there was not found a help meet for Adam. This implies that God searched among the existing created things, but he couldn't find anyone or anything that satisfied His need of a suitable help meet. So, God customized, designed, formed, and fashioned a woman to meet His desires, function, and capacity of serving as a help meet. You are God's solution to a problem; as a woman, you were created to meet a need, satisfy a desire, and you contain within you profound God-capacity to function for good where good did not exist in the earth.

Do you consider yourself a solution to a problem?

A WOMAN IS AT HER BEST WHEN SHE IS PROTECTING, SUPPORTING, AND BRINGING BALANCE TO HERSELF AND OTHERS

God spent detailed time thinking and creating woman because He designed her to be a help meet, someone who would bring harmony, unity, and diversity to Adam. Woman was a big deal for God to create. He didn't reach back into the ground, but He reached back into Adam to create Eve. In other words, Eve wasn't created from the ground, but she was created from God-breathed ground—she came from an anointed an appointed God-breathed man.

God created woman from a man's rib. Ribs protect three major organs: heart, lungs, and liver, the organs that help circulate blood and breath, which are essential to life. Woman was created from the essential side of a man, the place that provides protection, structural support, and purpose. Because a woman was created from a rib, this gives deep insight into how we are to function as women. We are protectors, supporters, and balancers in life. A woman is at her best when she is protecting the innocent, supporting the hurting, and bringing balance to life—all of this is bringing good to life, God's ultimate design for every woman.

There are several women in the Bible that brought good to the not good that existed in life by protecting the innocent, supporting the hurting, and bringing balance to the lives around them. One biblical woman that protected the innocent was Jochebed, Moses's mother. By hiding him from Pharaoh's unjust edict, she protected her innocent baby boy.

Another woman who supported the hurting was Pharaoh's daughter. She disobeyed her father's decree to kill Hebrew babies and supported baby Moses when she found him helplessly floating in the Nile River.

Lastly, we see Miriam, Moses's sister, who orchestrated and negotiated a contractual relationship with her mother and Pharaoh's daughter that brought provision and sustenance to Moses's life. Miriam's actions brought balance to life; she united the biological mother and the adopted mother to ensure that her baby brother would be fully loved, protected, well-fed, and nurtured in life. All these women used their voice to make the choice to bring good to the not good that existed in the earth. Let there be no doubt that when God created woman, he created her for good, to do good, and to be good in life.

GOD'S MASTER PLAN AND DESIGN IS FOR WOMEN TO PLACE THEIR FAITH, HOPE, AND TRUST IN HIM

Women today have turned away from God's master plan and design, which is to find their value, worth, and beauty in Him. Many women show up, pretty up, and listen up for men rather than for God. I don't believe that God ever desired for a woman to find her worth in anyone other than Him. When a woman places her worth and her value in a man's opinion, her worth and value can fluctuate in her mind based on changes in that man's opinion.

Men change, but God changes not. He is the same yesterday, today, and forevermore (see Malachi 3:6 and Hebrews 13:8). Many women seek to please men instead of God, and it produces anxiety, uncertainty, and insecurity. God's specific, detailed creation of woman speaks volumes of how He desires women to place their hope, faith, and trust in Him to live their best lives, give their best selves to Him, and thrive in life.

Week Two

Thought of the Week

---

*Because a woman was created in a place of rest and from
a man at rest, rest is essential to a woman's well-being*

People and things that steal your rest and pollute your peace come from
the enemy. Anxiety is a weapon often employed by the enemy.

DAILY REFLECTIONS

 A woman was created in a place of rest, the Garden of Eden. God didn't
create woman until after He brought order to the Garden of Eden.

Daily Takeaway: Order precedes rest

 A woman was created from a man at rest; God put Adam to sleep before
He created Eve.

**Daily Takeaway: Women are wired to rest; rest helps
women relate to God**

 A woman was birthed or brought forth in an environment of rest. When
God presented the woman to her new home and new hubby, there was
full and complete spiritual rest, financial rest, and physical rest for her.

Daily Takeaway: Rest is essential to a woman's well-being

Every woman has her own unique brand that God has given to her; it's her authenticity. A woman is strongest when she doesn't compromise who she was meant to be.

> **Daily Takeaway: A woman must rest in her God-given identity**

As the first woman's rest was challenged by the enemy, every woman's rest is at jeopardy.

The serpent challenged the woman's rest by causing her to doubt herself and God.

> **Daily Takeaway: Doubting yourself and God will give territory to the enemy**

As soon as the first woman made mental space for the enemy, she lost her liberty.

Women only remain free when they align their minds with God's divine calling.

> **Daily Takeaway: A woman's liberty is directly tied to abiding in God's calling.**

Determine what gives you rest and peace. Identify people and things that give you peace.

> **Daily Takeaway: Your rest is your responsibility**

Week Two

Summary and Reflection Questions

1. What happens to your mental and physical health when you don't have rest and peace?

....

....

....

2. Are there times you vividly remember being under overwhelming stress and anxiety? If so, describe how you felt, what you thought, and how you overcame the challenges?

....

....

....

3. Because the first woman was created in a place of rest and from a man at rest, do you think rest should be integrated in your life on a daily, monthly, and yearly basis? If so, how should it be integrated, and if not, why not?

....

....

....

4. What will you do to ensure you have the rest and peace you need daily, monthly, and annually?

....

....

....

5. List 3–5 activities that give you rest.

....

....

....

....

6. Do you agree that women are natural protectors, supporters, and balancers? Why or why not?

....

....

....

7. List the names of women who are or who have been protectors, supporters, and balancers in your life.

....

....

....

....

8. List 3–5 things you can start doing or stop doing to help support God's design and purpose for your life?

9. Have you ever found yourself more concerned about what man thinks than what God thinks?

10. Based on this week's teaching, have you drifted from God's design for your life? If so, how?

JOURNEY DEEPER INTO WOMANHOOD

Now that we have taken the time to look at ourselves and look at other women, Exercise 3 will allow us to review the similarities and differences we have with other women. Please remember our differences should enhance sisterhood not distract from it.

EXERCISE 3: Before you jump into week three, please take a moment to complete the simple exercise below. Review the chart and only circle *shared characteristics*, if you selected it for yourself and other women. Circle *not shared* if you selected a different characteristic for yourself and other women. Once you complete the chart, determine how many characteristics that were shared in both Exercises 1 and 2 for both you and other women. The characteristics you share with other women are the areas that allow for connection and growth, and the differences you share with other women allow for opportunity and education.

Example: if you selected **strong** for you and **strong** for other women, then mark that as a *shared* characteristic, if you selected **weak** for you and **strong** for other women, select *not shared*. If you have equal and/or more shared characteristics than unshared, you tend to see yourself like you see other women. If you have more not shared characteristics, you don't see yourself like you see other women.

How many characteristics were shared by you and other women?

Strong	☐ shared ☐ not shared	Weak	☐ shared ☐ not shared
Independent	☐ shared ☐ not shared	Dependent	☐ shared ☐ not shared
Kind	☐ shared ☐ not shared	Unkind	☐ shared ☐ not shared
Mature	☐ shared ☐ not shared	Immature	☐ shared ☐ not shared
Compassionate	☐ shared ☐ not shared	Indifferent	☐ shared ☐ not shared
Content	☐ shared ☐ not shared	Discontent	☐ shared ☐ not shared

Bold	☐ shared ☐ not shared	Fearful	☐ shared ☐ not shared
Connected	☐ shared ☐ not shared	Disconnected	☐ shared ☐ not shared
Authentic	☐ shared ☐ not shared	Conforming	☐ shared ☐ not shared
Collaborative	☐ shared ☐ not shared	Cautious	☐ shared ☐ not shared
Adventurous	☐ shared ☐ not shared	Reserved	☐ shared ☐ not shared
Flexible	☐ shared ☐ not shared	Rigid	☐ shared ☐ not shared
Restful	☐ shared ☐ not shared	Worried	☐ shared ☐ not shared
Respected	☐ shared ☐ not shared	Disrespected	☐ shared ☐ not shared

The Leave-Cleave Marriage Principle Benefits Women

Therefore shall a man leave his father and his mother, and shall cleave unto his wife: and they shall be one flesh. Genesis 2:24

A woman's worth in God's eyes requires a man to leave and cleave, which is walking away from his old life pattern and walking toward his new life pattern with his wife. God requires the man to leave some people in his past who have been valuable to him for a woman who will be of greater value to him for a lifetime. A man's parents can only take him so far, but a wife will do a man good all the days of her life, according to Proverbs 31:12. A wife in God's eyes is a priceless treasure that keeps giving more and more. You must note, the Leave-Cleave Principle was a prophetic calling on marriage by God. Adam didn't have a biological mother and father; God meant the leaving and cleaving for all future men who would enter holy matrimony.

The marriage principle of leaving and cleaving was given to man as a requirement for him to leave his family before he begins his new life with his wife. Additionally, women have physical and emotional peace when they have no rivals for their husbands' loyalty. Scripture supports this principle. When we examine past biblical patriarchs, we discover the following facts: Abram left his father's house, Jacob left Rebecca and Isaac, Joseph by default left and went to Egypt, and David left his father's house to become king. These men would have never fulfilled their God-given destinies had they refused to leave their father and mother and cleave to the new thing God set before them. A wife is a good thing and a new thing given to a man by God, and He requires total commitment to her in order to eliminate divided loyalties within a man's heart.

Many women apply the Leave-Cleave Principle to themselves and will leave their supportive families, long-standing friendships, and trans-forming faith, if they believe any of these relationships are interfering with their love of a man. God never meant for women to isolate, eliminate healthy relationships, and manipulate to get a man—this is backwards. A soon-to-be wife should not enter the sacrament of marriage, unless she sees her soon-to-be husband walk away from anything that could divide his loyalty from making her his priority. This shift in priorities must take place before the marriage begins, because it is an external sign of an inward reality. Once this shift happens, a woman can leave her parents and cleave to her husband and the two will become one in Christ. As women, we must stop making excuses for a man who is unwilling to walk away from some people and some things to be with us. If he can't, then he is not worthy of us.

It is important to understand that women who have entered into marriages with husbands who didn't follow the Leave-Cleave Principle—all is not lost. God can provide redemption, renewal, and restoration within marriages. But husbands and wives must be willing to walk into God's will and walk away from their own will to experience oneness in marriage as intended by this principle.

Genesis 2:24–25 states that a man shall leave his father and his mother and shall cleave unto his wife: and they shall be one flesh. If a man is unwilling to leave some people and some things for you, he is not worthy of you. This Scripture is profound for women because it reveals that a woman's worth is so substantial that God himself places a premium on it and requires a man to make a substantial sacrifice of leaving the old to cleave to the new.

A WIFE DESERVES UNDIVIDED LOYALTY

God understood the institution of marriage requires unrivaled loyalty. Additionally, God doesn't place this demand on a woman, but He places it on the man. This doesn't mean that women should allow their mothers and fathers to interfere in their marriages, but I believe many men have unhealthy attachments to their mothers and fathers which do interfere. God places this passage of Scripture to protect soon-to-be wives and gives them a barometer to gauge whether their soon-to-be husbands are ready for marriage.

If a man can't cut the apron strings of his mother and the need-to-please strings of his father, then he is not ready to be a God-fearing husband. Any woman who doesn't understand that she is worth a man's undivided loyalty, uncompromising devotion, and unequivocal love hasn't matured and truly is not ready for marriage. God himself has placed such a high value on a woman's worth that He requires her to be the center focus of a husband's life, by requiring him to leave his family and cleave to his wife.

God showed me before marriage that my husband's loyalties resided more with his mother and father than they did with me. I made excuses and ignored the leave-cleave marriage principle that God put in place to protect wives, and I reaped unhealthy and unholy consequences. I chose to ignore a marriage principle that God gifted women for protection, direction, and increase in life.

Wives are designed by God to be placed in environments that promote physical, emotional, and financial security. When Eve was given to Adam, she was placed within a peaceful, beautiful, and opulent garden. The Leave-Cleave Principle fosters emotional security and peace so wives may live at spiritual ease. It also promotes healthy self-worth and value because it is a God standard that ensures a strong marital foundation. Men who obey the principle understand the importance of a woman's value and dignity. Additionally, women who marry men who honor the principle have happier and healthier marriages.

Week Three

Thought of the Week

---

*A woman's worth and value are so high that God
requires a man to leave his mother and father and cleave
to his wife—a.k.a. the Leave-Cleave Marriage Principle*

*A man who is unwilling to walk away from some people
and some things to be with his wife is not worthy of a wife.*

DAILY REFLECTIONS

A woman's value is so high in God's eyes that He requires a man to leave his earthly mother and father and cleave to his new wife to have a new life in Christ. Marriage requires an ending of the old to begin the new.

Daily Takeaway: A man can't cleave to a wife if he won't leave his parents

The Leave–Cleave Principle is a law of marriage that makes it work. A man must walk toward his future with his wife and away from his past to have a new life.

Daily Takeaway: The Leave-Cleave Principle provides direction for a woman's future by creating singleness of heart with her husband.

A man must be willing to protect his wife's worth and value by placing her first in his life.

Daily Takeaway: The Leave-Cleave Principle provides protection for women

 The Leave-Cleave Principle gives wives whose husbands have failed to make them a priority the opportunity to get in alignment with God's standard for marriage while providing them with peace and security.

Daily Takeaway: The Leave-Cleave Principle provides correction for women

 A man must be willing to walk away from past patterns to walk into new things. A wife is a new thing that God gives to birth fruitfulness and dominion in a man's life.

Daily Takeaway: A good life with a good wife requires change

 A man who is unwilling to change directions with his loyalty from his parents to his wife hasn't matured for marriage. Marriage is for the mature not the immature.

Daily Takeaway: A man who is unwilling to change his loyalties in the direction of his wife is not worthy of a wife

 A woman who refuses to value herself the way God values her will suffer losses. A woman's worth can only be reduced or diminished by her.

Daily Takeaway: Every woman of God is worthy of a man's undivided loyalty, and she shouldn't diminish herself to be with a man that refuses to value her accordingly.

Week Three

Summary and Reflection Questions

1. If you are single (unmarried), do you feel you place the right amount of value on your self-worth? Why or why not?

2. Are you guilty of placing less value on your self-worth than God requires of you?

3. If you have failed to value yourself like God desires you to value yourself, what steps are you going to take moving forward to ensure you value you?

4. Do you believe when you devalue yourself it opens the door for others to devalue you?

....

....

....

5. Devaluing behavior may take on many forms and shapes, i.e., lack of respect in communications and demeaning remarks and actions. Give some examples of how you have devalued yourself and/or others?

....

....

....

6. Have you ever entered a relationship with someone who didn't place the proper value on your self-worth, and did you suffer because of it? If so, describe how you suffered—whether physically or emotionally.

....

....

....

7. Have you ever walked away from your faith to be with a man? If so, did the relationship work?

....

....

8. Have you ever walked away from your family or friends to be with a man who didn't walk away from theirs? If so, did the relationship work?

9. Why do you think God requires men to leave their mothers and fathers to cleave unto their wives?

10. How is God's design for a man's leaving and cleaving his parents tied to a woman's emotional and social health in marriage?

11. If you are married or have ever been married, did you place the right amount of value on your self-worth before you got married? Why or why not?

12. If you are married, do you feel you place the right amount of value on your self-worth within your marriage now?

13. Do you feel after you have been married for a long time it is too late to place the proper value on your self-worth? Why or why not?

14. Why do you feel it is so difficult for many women to accept that they are worth an unrivaled love by a man?

15. Why do you think many women spend so much time convincing a man of their unrivaled love and devotion for them and refuse to require the same in return for themselves?

16. Have you ever played yourself cheap or sold yourself short in a relationship? In other words, have you settled for less than the best you know you deserved (this could be personal or professional relationships)? If so, please explain.

17. On a scale of 1 to 10, how would you rate your self-worth and dignity, with 1 being unhealthy and 10 being healthy. Why did you choose this rating?

18. In what areas do you feel your self-worth suffers—professionally, spiritually, or mentally?

19. What steps can you take to improve your self-talk, so you don't self-sabotage or self-isolate?

A Woman's First Words Were the Words of God

E ve's voice changed the very course of humanity. "The woman said unto the serpent, We may eat of the fruit of the trees of the garden: But of the fruit of the tree which is in the midst of the garden, God hath said, Ye shall not eat of it, neither shall ye touch it, lest ye die" (Genesis 3:2–3). Eve was the first woman to preach the Word of God. Many may take offense to this statement, but when Eve proclaimed or preached God's words to the serpent the curse didn't exist on earth. There was no prohibition against women preaching that existed because God's equality reigned sovereign between man and woman. I submit to you that the prohibition against women preaching is a result of the curse that occurred in the beginning. When women use their voice to agree with God's purposes and plans they will experience the fullness of His promises without any negative consequences, because "the blessing of the Lord, it maketh rich, and He addeth no sorrow with it (Proverbs 10:22).

It is important to remember that a woman's voice is more than what she says, it is also what she believes and does. *Voice* has a comprehensive meaning. It encompasses more than speaking but also includes actions, attitudes, and beliefs. God intends women to use their voices in every aspect to align with Him. Women's voices were created to be powerful, purposeful, persuasive, perpetual, and pivotal to create change. This is why the enemy comes to distort, deceive, destroy, and delete your voice just as He did Eve's. There is power in every woman's voice, and when she uses her voice to align with God's, she is able to create the greatest good on earth.

After Eve ate the forbidden fruit from the tree, she used her voice to persuade her husband, Adam, to eat. Her voice was persuasive to convince, powerful to produce change, purposeful to create, and had a perpetual negative impact in the earth that continues today.

On the contrary, Mary's voice, the mother of Jesus, was powerful when she used it to agree with God (Luke 1:26–38). She used her voice to fulfill God's purpose and committed her heart to Him. Her voice has had a perpetual positive impact in the earth that continues today. Because she said yes to carry God's only-begotten Son, the gift of salvation was made available to everyone. A woman's voice when used in unity with God is pivotal to bring balance, beauty, and bountifulness to the earth, and when used contrary to God brings darkness, division, and death to the earth. Notice, when the devil wanted to destroy the world he came through a woman's voice, and when God wanted to redeem the world, he came through a woman's voice—The importance of a woman and her voice can't be denied.

Initially, Eve's voice was strong, secure, and aligned with God's Word (Genesis 3:2–3).

Her actions were certain. She spoke clearly, concisely, and convincingly. Look at what she said to the serpent. She stated that we don't eat the fruit, we don't touch the fruit, and if we do, we die from the fruit. This was a woman who was certain in her speech. Eve said what she meant, meant what she said, and acted accordingly. Eve's voice was in complete unity with what she believed.

EVERY WOMAN MUST GIRD THE LOINS OF HER MIND TO USE HER VOICE EFFECTIVELY

Before the enemy deceived Eve, she didn't eat the fruit, taste the fruit, or touch the fruit because she understood that she had to place both physical and mental boundaries in place to keep her in alignment with God's Word. Eve didn't dabble with sin—she stayed away from the fruit. Although God did not specifically say not to touch the fruit, I believe Eve's conscience told her that near proximity to the fruit was not in her best interest. She kept herself far away from sin so she wouldn't be tempted by it. The woman God created was intelligent, competent, and confident until she engaged in a conversation with the slithering, manipulative serpent.

Eve was protected, directed, and provided for by God as long as she rested in His will.

She was a woman to be reckoned with. Arguably, she was the most powerful woman in the world, not because she was wealthy, not because she was beautiful, not because she was the only woman in the world, but because she was a woman in the will of God. This is what we want as women. We want our voices to be in lockstep with God's Word, will, wisdom, and works in the world. The most powerful woman in the world is a woman in the will of God.

Why do we place more value on what the world says is valuable than what God says is valuable?

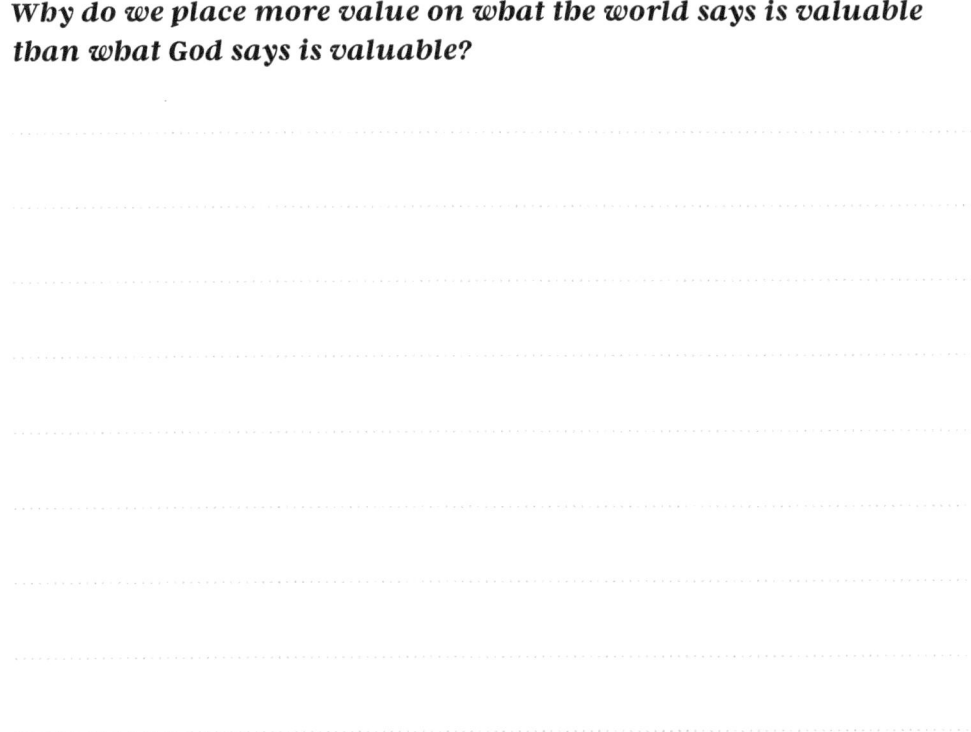

As a secure and strong woman, the enemy strategically attacked Eve's beliefs (which are a part of her voice) so he could weaken and ultimately defeat her. The only way Eve would falter, or fall, was if she stepped outside of God's Word, will, and wisdom. Thus, the enemy began his attack on Eve with a question of what she believed. The enemy's question seemed simple and innocent, but it was laced with deceit and lies. The enemy's goal was to replace God's voice with his lies, so his lies would be in the forefront of Eve's mind.

I don't believe Eve understood what a lie could and would do to her and her family. She was truly deceived. Women are deceived when they yield to temptation from an enemy. The Bible refers to the woman as the weaker vessel. Many women are simply weak like Eve, but the consequences of sin are the same regardless of whether you are weak or wicked. Thus, every woman must gird up the loins of her mind to ensure her conversations are aligned with God's will for her life (I Peter 1:13-16).

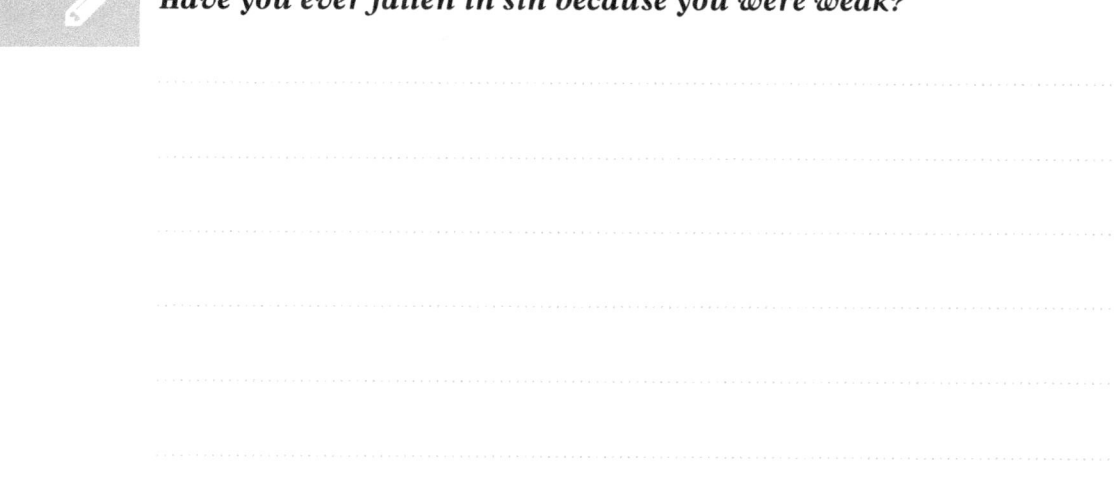

Have you ever fallen in sin because you were weak?

Genesis 3:16 states, "Unto the woman he said, I will greatly multiply thy sorrow and thy conception; in sorrow thou shalt bring forth children; and thy desire shall be to thy husband, and he shall rule over thee." This passage outlines the curse that rests on women's lives because of Eve's sin. Eve used her voice to align with the serpent's schemes instead of the Lord's plans. Remember, a woman's voice is also what she does as much as what she says. When Eve ate from the Tree of Knowledge of Good and Evil, she used her voice to agree with the enemy's plan, and it brought tragedy to her life.

The curse in Genesis 3:16 rests on women in their marriages and motherhood. These are the most important areas in many women's lives. Eve suffered emptiness not only in her marriage but her motherhood as well because of the curse. Cain killed Abel, and he was banished by God. As a mother, this caused Eve much sorrow. Additionally, Eve's marriage with Adam was forever changed when she convinced him to eat the fruit. The two were no longer the same and didn't share the oneness they knew before they ate the fruit.

Every woman after Eve has suffered in some shape, form, or fashion in their marriages and motherhood because the curse stood. Sarai was cursed in her marriage and her motherhood too. Abraham offered Sarai to both Pharaoh and Abimelech to save his own life, and if God hadn't intervened, Sarai would have been sexually compromised (Genesis 12:11–20; 20:1–10). Additionally, Sarai was barren for many years, and she suffered shame because she couldn't reproduce. But God broke that curse and rescued Sarai in both her marriage and her motherhood. God was the star of Sarai's story, and He will be the star of your story, too, if you allow Him to teach you.

Hagar suffered in her relationship with Abraham, and she also suffered in her motherhood because of Abraham. But God rescued Hagar as well. When Abraham put her out, God picked her up and took care of her and the child. Hagar's latter end in life was greater than her former (Genesis 21:14–21). Hagar's story teaches us that it does matter how you start, but it matters most how you finish. The curse of marriage and motherhood still stands, but it will not overtake you if you allow God's hand and His plans to stand in your life.

Week Four

Thought of the Week

The first words of a woman were the words of God.
A woman was the first preacher of the gospel.

DAILY REFLECTIONS

DAY 1

A woman's first words were the words of God. The first woman's voice was in alignment with God.

> **Daily Takeaway: A woman was the first person to speak the words of God**

DAY 2

The enemy was after the woman's voice from the time she came on the scene. He convinced her that if she ate from the tree she would be like a god. Eve failed to understand that she was already like God. She was made in His image and His likeness; she didn't need to eat the fruit. Just as God spoke the world into existence, Eve should have spoken her world into existence . . . not eaten her world into emptiness.

What Eve didn't understand is when she used her voice to agree with the enemy, she became less like God and lost some of her authenticity.

> **Daily Takeaway: A woman's voice is most powerful when what she believes, speaks, and does agree with God.**

A woman will use her voice to make choices. A woman's voice will bring her benefit or detriment; she decides what it will be.

Daily Takeaway: A woman's voice is most effective when she uses it to agree with God's plans and purposes for her life.

A woman's voice is more than words; it is also her beliefs and deeds. A woman's voice will bring equality and justice when used correctly.

Daily Takeaway: A woman's voice is designed to operate in authenticity

A woman who refuses to use her voice correctly will permit darkness to permeate inside. A woman's voice was designed to bring light, life, and liberty to herself and others.

Daily Takeaway: A woman's voice, when used correctly, brings light to life

A woman's voice is weakened when she fails to use it properly. A woman's voice will lose its power and impact when she refuses to trust God's design for her.

Daily Takeaway: A woman's voice, when used incorrectly, permits darkness to abide where God designed light

A woman's voice was designed to speak up, stand up, show up, huddle up, listen up, team up, and not give up, and God will reward her with a pay up in life. Every woman will break the curse off her life that traveled to her via Eve when she implements these 7-up principles.

Eve was supposed to speak up to the serpent, stand up to the serpent, show up authentically, huddle up with Adam, listen up to God, team up with Adam and God, and not give up on God's Word, and God would have caused a pay up in her life.

Unlike Eve, Mary used her voice to speak up and agree with God's plan for her life and stand up to the uncertainty that flooded her mind. Mary showed up to fully embrace the hard race she had to run as a virgin who would carry God's only-begotten Son. She listened up to Gabriel when He told her that the Holy Spirit would overshadow her to bring forth the child. Mary teamed up with Elizabeth, her cousin, to place herself in an environment of faith, family, and fidelity. She didn't give up on her marriage to Joseph, because she knew the very God who started the miracle in her heart would resolve Joseph's conflicted heart. God certainly rewarded Mary with a pay-up for her faithfulness; she is one of the most famous God-fearing women in history. Mary was created for good, to do good, and be good. Her legacy of goodness continually lives and serves as a model for all women that we can use our voice to bring continual good on earth.

Daily Takeaway: A woman's voice can change humanity for the better or the worse; it's her choice.

Week Four

Summary and Reflection Questions

1. Why do you think the enemy attacked the woman, Eve, instead of the man, Adam, in the Garden of Eden?

2. Why do you feel women are such a threat to the enemy?

3. Do you believe that all women will be attacked by the enemy so he can destroy their seeds in the form of children, businesses, books—anything that a woman can birth that will bring forth God's bountiful blessings in the earth?

4. Name a time you used your voice to align with God's purposes and plans.

5. If God spoke the world into existence, what do you think God designed women to speak into existence today?

6. How did Eve's voice change humanity?

7. How did Mary's voice change humanity?

8. How can you use your voice to change your world for good?

9. By eating the fruit, did Eve refuse to rely on her spiritual strength and rely on her intellectual strength?

10. Have you ever suffered a curse instead of a blessing in your marriage? If so, describe.

11. Have you ever suffered a curse instead of a blessing in your motherhood? If so, describe.

12. Can you list biblical or historical women who have suffered in their marriages or motherhood and God brought redemption?

....

....

....

JOURNEY DEEPER INTO WOMANHOOD

I think it is important that we spend time seeing ourselves correctly. If you see yourself as weak, you become weaker. If you see yourself as strong, you become stronger. It is important to identify the character traits you want to see in yourself and take steps to walk in them daily. If you want to be stronger, meditating on God's strength will help you get there, because His strength is made perfect in our weakness. In our final exercise, let's identify the character traits we want to see in ourselves.

EXERCISE 4: Congratulations on completing this study. Please take a moment to complete the simple exercise below to take a step closer to embodying the character traits you want to possess. Decide how you want to see yourself as a woman, how you want others to see you, and how you want to show up every day.

Example: Select one word from each column that embodies who you want to be, how you want others to see you, and how you want to show up daily. Refer to this list often and meditate on the character traits you want to possess.

How Do You Want to See Yourself?

☐ Strong 🍃 ☐ Weak   ☐ Connected 🍃 ☐ Disconnected

☐ Independent 🍃 ☐ Dependent   ☐ Authentic 🍃 ☐ Conforming

☐ Kind 🍃 ☐ Unkind   ☐ Collaborative 🍃 ☐ Cautious

☐ Mature 🍃 ☐ Immature   ☐ Adventurous 🍃 ☐ Reserved

☐ Compassionate 🍃 ☐ Indifferent   ☐ Flexible 🍃 ☐ Rigid

☐ Content 🍃 ☐ Discontent   ☐ Restful 🍃 ☐ Worried

☐ Bold 🍃 ☐ Fearful   ☐ Respected 🍃 ☐ Disrespected

Eve:
The Importance of a Woman and Her Voice

KEY PRINCIPLES

- A woman was created for good, to do good, and to be good in the earth.

- When the enemy decided to destroy the world, he did it through a woman—Eve.

- When God got ready to redeem the world, he came through a woman—Mary.

- Eve's voice changed the trajectory of humanity for the worse.

- Mary's voice changed the trajectory of humanity for the better.

- A woman walking in her God-given authority and authenticity is a woman who is powerful on purpose, for purpose, and helps others see their purpose.

- The first woman's voice, Eve's voice, convinced the first man to disobey God's plan.

- A woman's voice, Mary's voice, said yes to God's plan that brought forth salvation to man.

- A woman's voice is powerful, purposeful, pivotal, and persuasive in the earth.

- A woman's voice can be the difference between generational life and generational death.

- A woman's rest is her responsibility, and she must enter into rest daily to stay healthy.

- A man who is unwilling to walk away from his past into his present with his wife is not worthy of a wife.

- Women thrive with God-anointed and appointed men in their lives.

- A woman was the first person to speak the words of God.

- A woman's voice is strongest when her words, her beliefs, and her deeds all agree with God's.

Sisterhood of Womanhood Prayer

Lord, help me as your daughter and as a woman to understand my worth and value. Help me to place the appropriate significance on my life so I will not sell myself short, play myself cheap, or settle for less than your best for me. Help me to value other women according to their worth and not hide resentment, envy, or jealousy anywhere within me. Allow me to rest in my true authenticity and fully embrace my God-identity. Reveal to me how to use my voice to completely align with your will and word so I walk in total light and no darkness dwells in me.

I pray to walk in your divine power, divine anointing, and your divine appointing for me as a woman. Help me to lean into what you say to me and where you want me to be. Lord, I thank you that I am a woman of faith, grace, and endless possibility.

Final thoughts and an invitation to journey deeper into womanhood

God uses His Word to provide us with unsearchable life riches and treasures, and when we study His Word about women, He unlocks priceless wealth that helps women thrive and become better women.

Eve's story ends, but her impact doesn't. It is still felt among women today. If you have enjoyed this study, and want to learn more about the power of a woman and her voice, please secure your copy of *Sarah & Hagar: The Power of a Woman and Her Voice*. In part 2 of the Bite-Size Bible Studies for Women series, we will learn more about how Eve's mistake haunted the next generation of biblical women, but how God had a plan and has always been the champion, the deliverer, and the protector of women. Part 2 unveils hidden principles that educate, empower, and enlighten women to help mitigate the struggles and stresses they suffer in dating relationships, marriages, and motherhood.

About the Author

 **Catina Harris** is the women's pastor at Capital Christian Center in Sacramento, CA, where she ministers to thousands of women through prayer, Bible studies, and sisterhood circles. She is passionate about God's Word and sharing it with women in a way that allows them to see themselves as whole, healed, filled, and sealed by God's Spirit.

Catina works in full-time ministry, and she also works in corporate leadership in the healthcare industry. She has been married to her husband, Benjamin Harris, for over 18 years, and they have three beautiful teenage children. She homeschooled their children for six years, and she understands the weight and pressure that a woman faces and feels both inside and outside the home. Catina connects with women in real and practical ways. She champions women to stay in touch with their God-given dreams and passions and not to lose themselves regardless of the transitions they face.

Catina has a unique gift of highlighting the stories of God's daughters in the Bible that allow women to see the unseen and experience the wealth of God's wisdom for them. Women are liberated from faulty beliefs, self-sabotaging behavior, and untrue cultural standards that limit them. *Eve: The Importance of a Woman and Her Voice* will reveal why you are a **W**onderful, **O**pen, **M**eaningful, **A**ctuality (of God) **N**eeded (WOMAN) in the earth.